PSALMBOOK FOR THE WHITE BUTTERFLY

PSALMBOOK FOR THE WHITE BUTTERFLY

POEMS
BY
JAY BRADFORD FOWLER, JR.

1985
ORCHISES
WASHINGTON

Library of Congress Cataloguing in Publication Data

Fowler, Jay Bradford, Jr. 1951—

Psalmbook for the White Butterfly

I. Title II. Title: Psalmbook of the white butterfly.

PS3556.0843P7 1985 811'.54 85-2887

ISBN 0-914061-03-8

Some of the poems in this volume have appeared as follows: "Letter North" in Alan F. Pater's Anthology of Magazine Verse and Yearbook of American Poetry and before that in *Shenandoah*; "There Are No Bells In This House" in *Poet Lore*; "Deep In The Butterfly Body Of Love" and "What A Long Journey For A Woman Alone" in *Phoebe*; "Good Morning, Sister Corona" in *America*; "Letter Home" and "Free Fall" in *Gargoyle*; and "Dawn" in *The American Poetry Review*.

Cover drawing: Begoña Junquera.

Manufactured in the United States of America

Published by Orchises Press; 4831 Alton Place, N.W., Washington, D.C. 20016.

G 6 E 4 C 2 A

This book is dedicated to my mother and her mother, Ida Taylor, and to my father and his family up north, in Maine.

Contents

The Grandson

For Ida Taylor

Steering the body of the woman in white
Through the air down the hall
Into her last days, gliding evenly
Over the shining floor without touching
One square of tile. Changing myself into

Two hands, steering her disordered body
Down, past the orderly walls, the big
Windows full of snowing, in the childish
Home built out of bright blocks. My fingers
Radiating my love into the notched

Rubber handles, my childish love thinking
I could transmit through that
Steel chair, could open a vein in my palm
And thread my gleaming blood
Through the maze of the chair into

Her body and make her limp veins
Taut with the coursing. I wanted
To give my fingers as live nails for
Her bones. I wanted to connect
My nerves into her eyes. To blow

Into the vacant, stuttering bag
Of her heart. To have her rise
Out of the chair and walk away,
Back into the childish snowfall of her
Days, her hands pouring milk

Into the glasses of her children. Pouring
Higher and higher until the arc of white
Became a rainbow over the entire city
Where she would, that night, bend
Herself like a flower, over her childrens

Beds in her childrens rooms under the unquenchable
Rise of the moon, white like milk.

But I could not. I stood beside
Her body, in the wheelchair, by the window
And watched the sky raining all the
Whiteness out of Heaven onto the scrubbery
And the flat ground in the courtyard

In a white alarm and became her grandson
Down to the last burning and white and childish hair.

Letter North

I am so far south that it's as if, to be
A birch, a tree must have touched a unicorn.
I need to live in a deciduous forest,
To have the seasons bang doors like children.
But I also want the sea, fraying its waves on the
Backs of the rocks, bringing together the threads
Once again and miraculously rebinding them. One day
I shall really talk of the sea, but tonight I cannot.
It is the wind tonight that reminds me of waves.
The wind running down the mountains
To the sea in pursuit of the moon. Tonight
All the unicorns are dead. The birches grow
Extinct by the hour. It is the hour when I wash
The white scarves in the basement tubs, the scarves
I will wrap the birches in, telling myself—see,
These are the birches, they were touched by unicorns.
Washing, I think of north, where the unicorns
Move—in Maine, in New Hampshire. Bending, I am
Thinking of the trunks of the old birches that are
Broken and are seen from the highway—moving on,
Ruthless. The high branches brought low and the white
Bark clinging like lichen. I am thinking that maybe
This summer I shall drive to Maine. But now I shall
Sleep and when I awake the scarves will have
Grown cool and dry on the line.

When The Secret Taper Descends

When the secret taper descends
And holds steady on the tips of the phlox
Until they burst into blooms of pink
The man on the porch opens the door
To the yard and walks out into
The dark garden to hold his face among
Their blooms and smell their incense
And he can hear, through the still night,
The swinging incense canister of the bishop
Waved down the throat of the church.

The man comes back into the house
And writes: My body and my soul are my
Own. I inhale the phlox. Naked,
I bathe my body in the grass. My body
Is the garden. My soul in blossom I tempt
The butterfly. The night-time brings
A morning rain to wash the moonlight
Through all the trees of my arms.

When he begins to notice the apples
Green on the tree then the forsythia
Sprays are green and the grass and trees
Then Nancy's wash hangs on the line
And that night the scent of the green breeze
On their sheets and the man stays
Up into their night and he writes:

Their love binds them as the leaves
Are bound to the trees and as wide
As the sky their arms reach from
Horizon to horizon as their bed is
Their earth and the sun rises
And sets in their bodies. Their room
Is drawn into the morning like a tiny
Ship with curtains blowing and the
Breeze eddies around them until
They touch shore and awake.

When evening comes the shadows
Shudder about him and darkness
Begins to collect in the throats of the
Daylilies and color loses its voice.
Soon darkness will move on its silent
Hinges and close the garden except
For the lightening bugs appearing
And disappearing like thoughts, except
For the slow shift of the green
Trees always shifting yet never moving
And he will sit on the lounge
On the porch and write:

My hand crawls across the page,
In this faint light before dark,
Like another kind of garden animal
But soon I will set it loose
On my body and afterward
I will dream of the bishop, his ring
Glistening somewhere under this moon.
I will dream of my neighbors

Bending over their candle, but mostly
It shall be the fine circling
Edge of the moon that I shall
Sharpen my thoughts on, going round
And round. Loosing my voice trying
To practice my song that has no notes.

The Moon Has No Motion I Can Move

The moon has no motion I can move
Nor the trees in the night can I have
As my green leaves.

The moon made a soft motion
In the night and the leaves
Whispered closer to themselves.

My dream turns as softly
As the moon and thoughts, like leaves,
Grow in peace along their branches.

The moon is no maker. It does not mean.
And the leaves in the wind I cannot do.
The moon is no maker but for me to make

The letting of the moon grow soft
Upon my shoulder. The leaves are no wisdom.
They do not speak, but for saying
My prayers as I sleep.

In The Open Mirror

For Ida Taylor

No Smoking.
County Ordinance
Prohibits the Carrying
Of Lighted Tobacco
Products of Any Kind
Except In Designated Areas
—notice on the wall
in the nursing home

One bit of ash, that burned in secret
In the black face of my cigar,
Held to its glow as the nurse
Emptied the ashtray into the trash
And, just before it had eaten itself
Out, caught on the white edge
Of a birthday card and spread
Like a stain across the white
Space until it gradually ate the
Roses which blew up into a
Flame and passed slowly into other
Paper things until flames rose
In many points and the pink hairs on the
Robe that was laying on the chair
Picked up the fire and took it into
The robe until it ignited into one
Flame and burned like a mirage in the
Open mirror of Mrs. Taylor's compact.
And no one knew it. Not the

Two ladies in the room, asleep
On their nightly voyage on the oceanliner
With its hull drawing water in
Nightmare but which was drifting through
Fog toward the faraway Riviera
Of childhood where the sun
Burned like a ball that somehow
Was thrown too high and stuck, growing
Gold among streamers of cloud. No, no one
Knew it, not the one nurse dosing in the
Wheelchair in the hall, not the
Nurse at the station. Not the grandson
Who flew out of the place on
The wings of his health into the night
Sky of his solitude.

No one knew
Until almost everyone knew—when
Everyone who would wake up again
Was out in the snow or running or
Being wheeled out into the snow where
Firemen blew ice out of their hoses
Onto the home of fire where his
Grandmother still lay in the beautiful
Heart of the home and never woke
From her dream.

It had begun
For his grandmother as the warmth
Of simply lying under one too many
Blankets until she deepened in her
Dreams and imagined the warmth of
Hot chocolate on cold mornings in New York
As a child. Then it was suddenly

The first heat of the mornings in
New Orleans which would take her to
Open windows and which would send
Her by afternoon to close the shades
After the breeze had blown itself
Out. The she began to dream of
The influenza which hit the city and had,
Before she knew it, sent the hearses
Into the streets like cockroaches and she
Remembered the struck old man in
The next room in the boardinghouse and
How she piled armloads of blankets
On him. Then she began to truly burn
All through herself. It seemed as if she
Was being loosened, ascending
As she had watched the balloon
Ascend out of her fathers hand
When she was six and she had cried,
Jumping up, trying to fly, except that
This time she could fly, following the balloon.
She lifted off in her one dream
And rose out of the home of fire,
Above the people running around it,
And ascended into the high air, almost
Out of the winter now and then OUT
Into the place of stars and now OUT—
Beyond, where she rose to the balloon
And, smiling, brought her hands around it.

To Ben On His Sixth Month

To Benjamin Edward Cochran

Now, warming to the world
You sleep in the tremendous
Bed of a night in spring.

The house sleeps around
Your mother and father as they
Sleep on either side. You

Have not yet learned to
Sing or tie your shoes, but
Only watch the whirling

World and reach your mother's
Face, grabbing at her nose. You
Have not yet come to suck

Your thumb or be unwise
In love but here you are
All a wonder and being

Wise to warmth, playing
With your father's fingers,
Counting in the arithmetic

Of infancy, somehow you
Know the galaxy and all the
Fire of stars tightens

In your fist. Your mighty
Fist knocking on the
First doors, making your

Entrance into shoes and
Gloves and your first winter.
Your pink rabbit's foot

Body glowing with kisses
And your parent's faces
Moving like balloons on

Strings grasped by your
Fist. You have dimples for
Knuckles and new eyes

Where there will be old
Eyes. You have warm
Bones where there will be

Cold bones and all the
World opens and is wide in
Your wide, wide eyes.

Walking The Dead Land

For Jack and Carol

She raised the shade in the old
House and walked on the cold
Wooden floors. She had done what
There was to be done. She cooked for
Him, she read, and she sat alone

For a long time, especially in the afternoons.
But after this was over she lay down
And he went home and pulled down
The shade and walked the floors
And he lay down too, although not as

She had. He lay down and did not rise for
A long time. For the wind had died
Like a doe shot in the woods. He imagined
The doe's last breaths but they were soon gone.
The lung collapsed. The cold rushed in.

The house was left alone with its
Own sounds. It was settling as it was
Forever settling and he was settling
Around himself. The fine threads of the wind
Settled on his shoulders and in

That secret, only imaginable part of
Himself the sound of leaves which
The wind once carried was settling into
Him. And the sound of the birds that
The morning breeze blew in like light,

Ahead of the light, was flowing
Into his body which was so heavy with
Itself. All this took place when the
Wind died, and then he arose. He arose
After the wind had settled into his

Bones and closed the shutters. He
Arose to a world without wind and all
Was silent. He is walking his land. All
The trees are bare but in his body is
The sound of birds, that come before

The light and are like the light. In his
Ears are the sound of the trees riding
Out the wind. He is walking his dead land.
He is doing what there is to be done.
He knows the wind has died and that the wind

Is blowing. All this happened after she
Lay down. Whatever remains of her voice
Is flying then resting in the trees within
His bones, the shoulders of his soul
Upright and young. He is raising the shade,
Walking the house, doing what has to be done.

Christmas Poem

for Ida Taylor, age 92

Christmas in the home
Where all the bodies of injured butterflies
Are broken is not Christmas at all
But merely wheeling her
Through the halls painted a deaf grey
And past windows that arrive
Like ambulances carrying
A December afternoon.

But Christmas was in my fingers
As they stroked then patted the
Thick white sweater that covered
The flesh thinner than a butterflys wing—
Flesh that covered the veins moving
Into a blue sleep upon the
Bones melting into whiteness.

She asked me to put my tongue
In her mouth and grow words.
To put words in her ears
And to grow sound. To take
Out her eyes and rub them
Between my fingers so she might
See the warmth of Heaven.

But Christmas was not Christmas
And if God had been born
Then the huge wheels of her wheelchair
Were just two of the spoked cogs
In God's great brain and the
Crutches were the discarded
Legs of angels.

She wanted me to undress
Her there in the lobby. To remove
Her sweater, that thick skin,
And unbutton her dress and
Peel away her flesh, taking
Her bones away and letting
The small blood run. She wanted
Me to take her bare skull
And crack it under my arm.

But I could not and I could
Not take her home and I had
To go. I left in what was now
The miracle of my own walking
Out of the crumbling building.
I closed the door. My kingdom
Shuddered and I folded close
My wings.

The Poster

The gulls never leave
The rock. The sea

Is pinned to my wall. A white
Sun burns in gold
Clouds. The rocks

Are black. The waves
Never move. One sail,
Like a point of rock, does not

Glide. There I am, not
Walking on that beach.
Caught, in a picture place,

I think to pull down the
Shreds of cloud. Always

Never moving, I think to scare
The gulls, swim out
To that rock, climbing

The waves with my arms.
I think to leave, though I am
Captured in a point of departure,

Always about to leave, but,
Finally, too diminished to go.

One Long Pillow For The River

Here there are too many faces—
The face of the moon, blank
With light, uttering no
                    psalm.
The huge, terrifying face
Of the sky, mournful with clouds.
Filled with the cries of
Dying stars. My
                Palms—
Filled with the wounds of sky
Ropes. The faces of my fingers, pink
            And smooth. Here, also,
Are too many sighs in the deep belly
Of passion that should be
                        Singing. Trees
Asleep in February—their arms
Frozen in the midst and shape of passion. Birds
Without nests. The whole wide
                            Waits
For an arrow to be driven into
Its heart. Almost nowhere, I come
            Listening. Paying my
Attention to the many faces and the sighs
And the sky, now asleep. I am
                Going to make
A prayer out of wood—an empty
Birdhouse. I am going to find
                            A place
And lie down, like snow, and be cold.

I am about to knit
A sweater for the wind. A warm hat
For the mountains. A great scarf
For the trees. One long pillow
For the river. Come to meet me here, halfway
Between two sleeps, moving through the
Groggy
Destiny of one flung man falling,
Slowly through the kind-hearted
Evening in the inpenetrable heart of
The perfectly empty
World
Lifting its body in the unhappy man and
Moving its limbs in all things, forsaken
Or not. Now he comes, forshaken and
Apart
From love and the willow—dipping
Its leaves in the streams of summer. Most
Afraid of the interminable daylight
Come to bring him long rivers
Without pillows and bareheaded
Mountains
To climb and the crowded window
Of things, filled with faces.

Good Morning, Sister Corona

Yes, Sister Corona,
You are smiling

And so are the
Scrambled eggs, smiling
Yellow. You are real

And simple as in a storybook
And suddenly the
Storybooks are real as

This fat hospital, smoking
Its short stacks. As real
As the colors of the trees—

All deep green and burgundy—
The colors of the heart.

You are real Sister Corona.
Good morning and thank-you.

Free Fall

1.

Not steadied by my hand
Will the moon ascend. Nor will the stars
Shine because my two eyes peer.
The trees will not throw down their
Cloaks because I cast my shadow
Into shadows. We move separately and I dwell
Where star does not lift nor moon
Make white so round. No star
Sees me where I go and go. No moon
Runs around me where I shine unknown
To woman, man or morning.

2.

Unbidden I come—called only by
My fear of night. Dreams
Hang like stones about
My neck. They want to be buried.
Blood starts at every pore
And my veins breathe in a
Hurry about my skull seeking
Detonation. The journey I would split
With a stone—its veins coiling like
Serpents in my wrist. The blood I would drop
In the grave and not sack it about
Over my cruel bones and be and be.
The shadow of my bones I would
Spread over the dark water
Like a crucifix. The dark water!
Rubbing its palms together
After me, smoothly.

Valentine Poem—Memories Of Being Someone Else

(to the little blind girl in the basement)

1.

Come a long
Way without words
To deliver my valentine
To the stillborn
Children
          Waiting
By the hospital incinerator.
                              To
The children at the
School for the deaf where
I played piano
                    On
New Years Eve.
Be mine. Be mine.
Be mine in sleep. Mine
In dream. In sleep
And dream be
Mine.
                         Come
A long way through
Great trial to let this
Cripple dance
On the table, in love
With the moon.

2.

In Montrose park—
Across the street
From the school for the
Blind we crossed
The dew
And lay down, making
Love.
        Hardly
Did I get a hold. My handle
Was more the moon, coming
Apart in the sky.
                        Who
Was I, cradled in someone's
Arms. I am not cradled
Now. Only
A candle in my
Body—I burn
Alive.
        Memories
Of being someone else
Fill my body
With mysterious
Bones. Strange
Muscles contract in my
Thighs. Where
Am I walking?
And the wine of someone elses
Nights of talk move
Through my heart.

3.

Nights I ascend—
A choral master for the mute.
My arms in the air
I meet the world.
I say
To the blind and the dumb
and the deaf—once I
Saw and spoke, once I heard
And once the moon
undressed for me. But
They know everyone
Has memories of being someone else.
Tonight the moon
Is undressing
In the winter garden. Much
I think of the moon
But little of Jesus. Rather, I wake
To hear the winter sparrows
And I roll the stones.
Happy,
In the nights, I fuck
The moon. I forget
To say my prayers to the blind
But here I
Am, quite
Deaf and dumb and quite blind tonight, writing
My valentine to
My neighbors, dreaming
Of being
Someone else.
Be mine.

To Margaret And Her Family

Your brother's son is weary. His flesh
Is burning but his bones are cold.
Gently, by the wrists, he was once
Asked down, to lie in the grass.
The summer moon in the sky. Now
By sleep—the yoke of stones stooping
His shoulders, he is brought flat.
He knows that he knows he sleeps
On the same bed as all of you—
Sleeping inland away from the seas cold breath.
He knows but is uncertain, the way,
Up close, the color of your Maine
Birch is uncertain, Walking,
In the same light as all of you
I see our lives are bent, differantly,
Round our fingers, like bits of grass. They
Are jostled in our mouths by our
Differant tongues. And in winter,
When we, like sparrows, inhabit the trees,
It is each in our differant dream.
Each of us has delayed in arms that were
Not ours. Each of our houses trembled
In the wind and we moved our center in.
But where we lie down it is all
Uncertain like the color of the birch.
Where we lie down, far inland, from
The same uncertain but cold and colorless sea.

❁ ❁
❁

Once
The world was on its feet
And singing.
Now
I do not dream. My
Heart, sucked, dry as a flower, does not
Think to fall. Does not care, thinking
Of spring
And the moist, the
Most green world. Unbelieving, I do
Not think to bring
The vases out into the yard and fill
Them with moonlight. I do not
Think to weep
Unforgiving tears. Feeling first,
I fell through the world. Amazed,
I forgot to be cruel. Here I am,
My sea
Beating
On no shore I ever saw. Not
Held between the beak of a beautiful,
Dangerous bird, my ribs crushed, do
I rise. I rise
Destroyed, out of my time, split
Off from my only seconds. Come
To this cage to see this
Man
Searching his body, his pocket. Up to
His elbows in his ribs he wants
To love again—
Unutterably ill, in
Love, he wants
To be.

I do not forgive the round
World or the people or the many
Flowers or the slight
Veil of frost I woke to on Sunday
Mornings, hung with bells.
Ungiving, I gave
The most of me—the trees, full of
Wind
And the dahlias I grew, big as kisses,
Exploding around your face in the photograph.
Going now,
I smile,
The host on my tongue, I go
Into my times time, with the moon
And the aging stars and my boots
In my words. Having nothing to
Do
With petals, I do not sip
The wine from the cracked chalice
Of the rose, having already given
My body to the roses, my legs and
My brain
And the unknown center where my
Tears
Wash and my sorrow dress and my
Rainbows dive, headlong into the sea.
Unglorying
The world, I give up, not wanting
To touch the insignificant rest
Of my making good the tall
Story
Of the world, trees in love, rocking
The continent in summer, when the birds
Sing and the apples rise. The best

Found its way out of the world, out of my
Music I walk away from the least and
Last
Stumbling down. I hate the fat moon
That falls tonight, on the backs of lovers
And the thickening bud filled with
The blood of sorrowing love.
I could
Yet be lucky with death—
Soon, in the murdering world.
It would please
Something in me to mash the ongoing,
Perplexing,
Rise of the beautiful moon, coming, steady
Through the nights. It would tickle
A rib
To die
Bad. But mostly I am already
Gone
Unwed and too alone to be found
And made awake, all in glory, remade,
Poisoned
With new love and full of grace. Ungotten,
I give back the moon and the child-faced
Roar of spring, and the
Greedy man and the good man in me, crossing out
The many entrances into light. I give back
My love.

Letter Home

To Ian Macrae

The night cuts through the park like a train
With a long haul of empty boxcars, going west.
I sit beneath the trellis where I once
Dragged the deep pool in the creek
For my bones. Now I turn to other things.
This summer I shall move to the beach because
My heart grinds out sand and my veins return it
With sound of gulls. I shall travel by bus
To the indescribable color of the waves.
I shall rent a place as close to the beach
As the first bunches of grass and sit calmly on the porch
Drinking, as the sea runs itself out towards my house
Like a whale's tongue. The wine will fill by body
And my organs will float inside me like fish.
My backbone wash up on a lost shore, each vertebra
Another knot in the storyline. Come
To see me at the beach, where the sea
Washes itself over and over again and turns
Up white. Come to sit with me and we shall
Talk about the uncertain color of the sea
In our eyes and the grass ebbing slowly away
From the water. We shall talk til moonlight
And then we shall see the broad and slight
And moonlit backbones washed up by the tide.

Do Not Ask Me About The Sun

Do not ask me about the sun.
I only know the sun rounds the sky
In a rainbow's arc

But I cannot creep through
The opening that is the world
And each horizon is an enemy of mine.

Do not ask me about the sun
But let us exchange gifts—
I will give you the skyline,

The ragged edges of the trees
And I would like for you to give
A kettle to boil water for tea

So we can sit and talk and I can
Tell you: do not aske me about the birds.
I only know they start at four o'clock

To sing. But when they die
I cannot take one small bone
With me to eternity.

Let us walk through the field
Behind the house but do not ask me
About the trees. I only know

They stand by the river
Like refugees waiting for a train,
Then the plague of frost turns them mad

And they fling down their leaves
Like diamonds on the grass
And the earth, the earth

Bites each one to pieces. Do not ask
Do not ask, just let us walk
Beneath the trees and hear

The murmuring of children, cupped
Hands in the water and eyes
Turned towards the sun.

Now let us follow the streams
To the hill and climb to the meadow
Surrounded by trees that cling

To the sides of the hill
And hold the circle of green
Grass together, hold the empty space,

The silence where the sun beats
Mercilessly and when we sit to rest
Do not ask about the field

Because I only know
That my answers revolve
Around an empty space

Where I circle like the trees
The lack of, where the sun
Beats down, beats down forever

And the talk of the trees
And the wind is a tireless
Haggling about the riddle

Of the field and that when
I go I shall have gone
Talking myself to death.

❁ ❁
❁

What the sun and moon can do together
Does not surprise me.
I want to die.
                    Lay
My body down. I do not want
To moan all night in the tremendous
Bed of spring. The grass
                                        Moans
All summer long in the fields. Not
By the magnificant trees
Do I go. Nor by the summer streams
Bending
Their way into
Heaven. That much has
                                        Passed
Away. I do not dream. Lord,
It is time for death,
Not prayer. A prayer to
Be dead coils and beats
Its fists. Beating
                        My fists
I make my way. I do not go
As if my body was full of
Flowers. I do not want
To meet the many
Seasons meeting
                        In the vortex
Of my soul. Here
Is the hiatus in the
The storn. I press the dead
Center of the dream
                                unto
My breast.

There
Is a tombstone in the sigh
I have to plant
                    in the secret
Hearts of graveyards—a world
Full of tombs, I lift the shade
In the unwelcome room.
                              Pressing
My eyeballs into the lips of death
How do I contend? How do I weep?
Here comes now the whole hill
                                        Like a
                                   Hearse
Bearing a load of houses. I have to shut
My thighs. Lifting your scent off
My fingers like an impression of Christ
I smell my way, in love in the
Unpardonable
World. Come to see
                         me here, where I lift
My voice, high up
Through the risky
                    Air
In a dumbwaiter come somewhere
Out of the dark and traveling
Through the sky towards Gods
                                        legendary
And perfect and irreparable
                                   love.

Worst by worst
Way I have to make
My way. Here, in this winter,
The children ride
by
On bicycles. I have to keep
Myself thinking there is
Blood in those
bones, babies
In my little purse of sperm. But
Finally I do not believe
The tall stories of my
Lover—the lilac. She is
So sweet and purple.
I hear
Her swing her load of blossoms
Into spring. I hear
Her sing from the unreadable
Psalmbook of the spring.
I am
Begotten by nowhere
And I see
No need to weep
The strange
Tears
Of love. Out of love I do not mourn.
But, now it comes to me——Lover,
I call myself out and by
Name. There is a phantom
In this
Kiss.

The Second Bob's Diner Poem

So now it comes to me,
As I sit in this fat
Diner, putting a lump in

My belly, how your love
Became a slipper I put on
And walked the heels

Out of the night. How everything
Changes and how everything
We touch becomes what we

Have touched and we run
Our course. Tonight the slipper
Will wait by my bed

Like a cab, a yellow
Cab that waits by this
Diner's door.

A Straight Line Of Love

My father will not ascend into heaven.
He will drive there in his Packard.
And the drive will be north, through
Connecticut and New Hampshire, to Maine,
And beyond. One night my father will rise
From his bed and leave the little
Room with the chest of drawers and its wild
Garden of photographs—the four sided
Family memories cut out of the Maine
Woods and sky. The memories with walls and
Rugs and chairs when he needed a place
To sit. And woods and gates to the mansions
of the rich folk when he needed a place to drive.
  earth and sky when he needed a
Place to run or stand. That black and white
And mostly a fine gray garden where
The woods would explode into green beneath
His fingers and dust would settle once again
On inland country roads. My father will leave
That room and leave our house and climb
Into the waiting Packard remembering
Once again when he was three and sitting
On the running board of his father's 1913 Buick
With his back, straight as Maine, against the door.
He will keep to a straight line of love
Along the winding shore roads
That play with the sea. He will put it
Into high running out through the big
Potato fields in blossom. And the angels

Will first catch sight of his white
Roadsters scarf as he rounds the last
Bend and drives up the
Sunny road to step off into glory
On a dazzling summer day. Mary
Will be there to greet him with the
Neighbors and their children and they
Will all invite him to stay for dinner
And to shake his Father's hand.

There Are No Bells In This House

There are no bells in this house.
Only the big bell of night—
We hear the moon ring.
You will know no bells here,
Only the bell shaped blossoms
Of the snowdrop, though their shape
Is one of prayer, not song.
There are no bells in this house
Or at least not the bell
You strained to hear. There are
No bells here, though your words
Strike like notes and your hand
Moves across the page like a bell
Swinging. There are no bells
I tell you, though the snowdrops praying
Broke a big bell, shattering
The irretrievable note of winter.
There are no bells in this house
But all the bells are beating—
The moon gong pounding roundness
Into roundness, the night shaking,
And the snowdrops deafness
Sounding whiteness hooded onto
Whiteness—now all the bells
Are battering and the snowdrops
Deafness is poured into the moons
Roundness. But there are not bells here.
Only the moon drunk on its own whiteness.
Only the snowdrops drowsy in snow.
Just the sentences wagging loose, off.

Moving, At Last

Unutterably white he made
A death. Not to be mourned
And gradually forgotten had he
Lay down. Nor had he lived
To be consumed, hour by hour,
Through the gradual day.
His body he left like a note
On the incredibly white ice
Below the traffic traveling
Through the sky. Always quite
Ready to die he had arisen
To the bridge on the rungs
Of limbs through the trees he climbed
As a child and somersaulted
On his feet and hands to the death.
Alive, he was nowhere at rest
But always wanting to be under
The snow or the blankets of spring.
The world crushed in his hand—
A fragile egg, hardly born
But singing. For the sea he walked
To the sea but this he did
For himself, in love. In collision
With the stars he fell, past
The universe and the play ground
Out back and his mother's cries.
He did not kiss his mother
Or the world good-bye. He did not

Think to mourn the tree,
Though, filled with green
Echoes, he fell
Out of the treehouse. Sadly,
In the pitch of night, he
Forgot to be dark, but sang,
Happy, to be moving, at last,
Out. The ice was pure,
A clean page to compose,
Not in terror but with
Purpose. Illegibly, mourning,
He had made his way, but
Now he would say and
Stay to the point. Happy, at
Last, he had sailed down
To the river, where he could
Not dream.
                    Dead, at last,
Under the good stars, he would
Sail out to sea on a piece
Of ice that would dissolve,
Like the Eucharist, on the dark
Tongue of the Atlantic. Sailing,
Down through the clear air
To the ice that separated his
Head from his body and scattered
His arms and legs, to lie
Like the body of a butterfly,
Without wings. Nailed by
The fall, he lay like
A short match, below
The city, smoldering with
Light. Flat, he had leveled

Everything, no longer to burn
In the hot world, alive.
Slowly, the water fell out
Of the mountains west of
Him and pushed his sleeping
River seaward. The loud world
Was no longer in his ears,
And his body soaked up
The cold, echoing blood.
Safe, to be here in the
Unhurtful world, the uneventful
Sky and the trees wading
Into the ice. Happy not to
Be halfway here anymore
He would not lie down
Without love, but instead,
Merely not be. Head first,
He had knocked his head clear
Of his spine and destroyed
That union he had always
Known. No longer put
Together he would no longer
Walk within the circle
Of summer and wear
No ring. All the way down
I think he smiled.

What A Long Journey For A Woman Alone

1.

When he was a boy
His grandmother's cane
Would lie
Harmlessly
Among the light
and conversation.

But at night
When he was close
To sleep, he would always
Hear it walking and stamping
On the floor
Above him. He would dream
Of the one-legged
Man in the movie. He knew
That unlike the others, who would
Merely drown, he would be
Eaten by the whale
All white.

The neighbors would come
Back to his house
After church on Sundays
The days that were white
With bells and doilies.
His grandmother could barely
Hear a word they said
And she would sit by her coffee
And merely smile
When someone spoke to her.

He use to see the corners
Of her mouth, the part that makes a smile,
Turn black. White butterflys
Would come to feed upon
Her there, carrying bits
Of lip away.

He used to dream
That one night in the summer
His parents went to her in their
Sleep. They wrapped her in gauze,
She was so frail and white.
They took her down
To the field by the pond
And made a hole
For her. They stoned
Her with handfuls
Of miraculous darkness
And when it fell
It fell through
Her. They filled the hole
And went back
To their room. They locked
Each other in their
Arms.

In his dream
Next Sunday and the neighbors
Would come. They would
Ask about the old woman
Who sat by her coffee
And his parents would always say
She has gone back
To Utah. She took the train

Just last Friday.
And everyone would toll
What a long journey for a woman
Alone.

He used to watch
His mother put on her
Heavy garden gloves
And go out to attack
The wild thistles
That rose above the garden.
She would burn them
Afterward. From inside
The house he used to hear
His father's shears chopping
The shrubs. Always he would
Cut them into stiff, formal
Shapes. He would go after
A twig like a woman
Quickly straightening a stray hair.
He began to wonder if they
Too were aware of the white
Butterflies and if bits of their
Dreams drove them to attack.

In his dream
They had put her too close
To the big pond where he
Was never supposed to play.
But one afternoon he went
Down there, leaving his grandmother

To sit on the porch, the wind softly
Tugging her hair and playing
In her clothes.
The trees by the pond
Were covered with white
Butterflies and he went down
To the water and looked in.
Her face smiled up at him
With the same smile she used
On Sundays. Minnows flowed
In and out of the darkness
Of her mouth.

He knew then that the big
Whale that would eat him
Would come from his grandmother's
Mouth. He knew why the pond
Was forbidden and why in his dream
They had locked each other
In their arms.

Soon after that day
He began staring
At his grandmother's cane.
It was like listening to the locusts
At night. He never tired of it.
It was shined with years
Of a bad leg and it grew brighter
With each passing
Day. After years of schooling
By his grandmother's side
He became blinded.

All he could see and hear
Was what he remembered
And all he could remember
Was the walking and stamping
And the white butterflies.
All he could remember
Was his grandmother's face
Where his should have been.

2.

As a man
He writes: I wait.
I wait with the wind combing
My hair out, the cane
Waiting by my bad leg
As constant as the song
Of the locusts.

I wait. On the ponds
Bottom my mouth gives
Birth to whales. Children
Come to see minnows swim
In my mouth. They run home
And years later
They write legends about a time
Of whales all white.

Little children,
Whatever age you are,
Do not peer into the legend
Of your pond's bottom
Unless you would see
The whale making legends
Out of your days.

The Winthrop Fragment

Up north, in Maine, this time of year,
The sky draws up the shade and the sun
Shines down. My father's folks
Bring their cold bones out in burlap bundles
They open on the grass. They arrange
In the sunlight, the bones that January
Walked into February with, the legs
Of snow. They count their ribs, where
The heart in winter danced like a squirrel
Then curled up to sleep with a nut in its
Cheek and its face in its tail. They sit
In a circle with their skulls in their laps
And rub the bald bone warm.

Margaret, my aunt, goes in to get coffee.
Once she had a house with windows
All around. It was anchored, like her life,
By the lake it looked out on. But she
Unwound its rope and it drifted into
The neighbor's back pasture where the cows,
Each summer, grew rooted in the fields.
Everyone who knew Margaret will remember
The windows and how her life slipped and
The house and how it drifted into pasture after
Pasture and finally disappeared. Now she lives
In a trailer with her husband, Charlie, and they
Sit on the grass with another winter's
Bones while Harold, her brother, makes coffee.

Charlie picks up the bones of Margaret's
Fingers and rolls them in his own warm hands.
He does not want her to count anymore.
She counts over and over and he wants her
Fingers to rest and be warm, though
He himself raises out of her bones
Child after child in his arms. They who broke
Through the fragile hymen of darkness
Into light, but only for awhile, and
Now she counts all day and all night
The children whose bones were not once
Warmed out of a winter.

Her house still has many windows
But now each one is a dead child's
Eye. All night the doors of the bedrooms
Open and close. They walk the upstairs. From
The window she can hear one of them
Screaming from the creek. He is drowning.
She awakes, then tries not to disturb
Her husband who is playing, laughing with
His boys, his girls, walking the meadow
Path of the creek, now driving the car
To the ice cream stand by the lake.

Today, husband and wife, they have come over
To my uncle Harold's house. Now all three
Of them are placing their bones back in the
Burlap. But they are sleepy with the
Afternoon sun and Margaret lifts her brother
Harold's bad foot into her own pile of bones
And Margaret's pelvic bone is placed in her
Husbands bag and all of their fingers
Are mixed, before they leave.

Deep In The Butterfly Body Of Love

To Helen Lessenger

It was morning now and raining.
The man got up from the desk
And went to the window to look
On the garden where green
Leaves had rained down on the
Trees months ago and he could
Feel the tiredness growing
In the smallest twigs, that
Invisible frost climbing down
The branches to grab the trunk
And shake. He looked out on
The garden and then he went
Back and wrote:

The bees slept all night in
The blossoms of the phlox,
But I do not know if they are
There now. And the white
Butterflies that inhabit the
Garden are not there in the rain.
I do not know where they sleep.
But I do know the phlox blossoms
Are sewn on with the thread
From the gut of the butterfly
And out of the body of love
All things can be drawn
As the morning is drawn following
The scent of butterflies into
The garden. But when the
Butterfly folds its wings

Into flakes of snow why must
I fold winter's book of whiteness
Alone, why must I ask—
Is the butterfly alone?

The man slept that day
And when he rose in the early
Evening he went to sit on the
Porch. There was another
Thunderstorm. With the rain
Came an early night and the
Darkness flowed into the porch
Like a tide. He turned on the
Lamp and in the harsh light
He wrote:

I hope when you read
This autopsy, when you open
My brain, the scent of phlox
Will fill your room; and when
You press your finger against
The cells you will find the
Butterfly that rests gently on
The phlox, still as the blossom
In the heat, while summer
Sleeps wide eyed and slows down
Like a child's swing. I hope
You find the world becoming more
Of itself, as if the lightning bugs
Did not have to rise with evening
And the garden not be shuttered
With night, as if the moon

Did not have to appear like a
Skull in a web of stars and I
Did not have to walk out into the
Garden, and open a brown, curled
Leaf to find a buttefly asleep
For as long as the moon would
Appear faceless above the trees.

He lay down on the couch
And fell asleep. He dreamed
The only dream—the time when
The world stopped revolving
Long enough to get a string around
The sky and play it out like a
Kite, to feel that tug and tug—
She tugging his hand as they
Walked down the hill where the
Clover waded through the grass
With white lanterns, always going
In whatever direction they went.
He dreamed the sun went down
Behind the trees, leaving the park,
And the night came behind a moon
That grew tighter and tighter in
Its roundness, in its whiteness,
Until they pushed from one another
And lay alone side by side, the
Tiny clover lost in the darkness
And the rungs of its lamps too
Small to pick up the light of the moon.
Later, after the moon had fallen
Asleep in its whiteness, they
Smoked and talked. The leaves were

Startled again and again by the
Breeze and the dew quieted the
Whispers of the grass. He dreamed
That when he went home that night
He sat down at the table and wrote:

In the clothes that I put on
Again in the park are bits
Of dark soil, and if I shake
Them out I am afraid the brains
Will fall out of my bones and I
Will have to forget how to even walk
Out of the park alone, side by
Side. If I shake my clothes I am
Afraid the grass I collected
Will fall and plant my memories
Into great trees that I can only
Walk beneath and all will be
Changed when I awake. I am afraid
To wipe the dew from my eyes
Because the brown of the iris
Will run and I will be rinsed of
Even your face and the tiny clover
I do not understand but I know
Is lost. Lost beneath a moon that
Is shattered, wrinkled with
Blackness, old and adrift. It light
Wandering senseless through woods.
I am afraid to speak, because my
Tongue would try to crawl back
Beyond its root, back to the
Unutterable where I live with the
Moon, not her; where I lie down

With the grass, not her; the
Unutterable that rises without a
Note into song, into light.

In the morning he awoke from
His dream. He was sad he had not sat
Up with The garden and gone out
To have the minutes buried with
The fragrance of the phlox or
Stood in the yard alone wishing
He was the white birch, so he
Could shine white in the moonlight.
He was sad and he got up and wrote:

The night passed through my sleep
Like a falling leaf. Here in the
Staring face of morning, here in
The green glances of leaf, in the
Glaring sun; here in the morning,
There is nothing of the whispers of
The two of us, once so perennial
In the nights that we did not even
Have to be there. Here in the
Morning, there is no poem except
The verse of absence and something
In these lines, something in the
Darkness of the ink of these words,
Tells me last night was the last
Night of summer and I was not awake.
Today the blossom head of the
Pink phlox are ragged, green with
Seeds. Something in that greenness,
That going back to green, tells me
They are spent.

Last night when the moon
Lay buried in cloud, last night
Deep in the hours, the petals
Of the phlox rose from their stems
And floated over their branches.
The night winked and in that time
A few of them, just enough to
Tow the moon, just enough to spin
The world, a few of them changed
Into white butterflies and took
Flight, just enough to keep the
Clouds flying, to keep the
Clouds white.

In autumn the butterflies do not
Leave the world through the horizon
Like the birds. They do not fall
And die on the ground like the leaves
While the rain pounds the color out
Of their fans. They do not enter into
The flesh of branches and sleep
In the roots of our sycamore, our
Oak. Rather, they winter in whenever
We ask—Where do the white butterflies
Sleep, sleep through the cold?

Dawn

1.
after the painful tuning for the song,
  after the dog sounds,
the feverish legs in the long wool socks,
  the pushing off at midnight, fog
calls, crossings from the kitchen, kisses
  from deep coats, an Atlantic poem, after
the music of the lights, the cherished
  small life, the ache that seems alive
  in the thermal house, after these
    there will be

2. the open boat,
  the exorcism of the pig-eyed lights
  the painful florescence, slaying of the animal —
his huge dark side, the sacrifice of this
  time, devastation, soon, of the moon cropped
    fields and hours, kill of the squirrel black —
all this by the blue swarthe, the healing
  bandage, ointment of color, the ring in
the upstairs out of doors, O the hand on
  the latch of the gate, flower to my wrist, love
  in the midst, visitation, her gown on
  the stair window frames, until we step
    on the open boat

3.

without reluctance, at last
the shift from the natural, ride up to the rail
to climb on the water with a wing, the melting
of suave before the sun
is there
like a burning
crucifix, like a gull we watch like
a mountain turning into a flower,
the fruition of a destiny, coming alive
for a child, like a poem in a book of psalms
we know we could write if we
could die, like the final emptiness
that is pulse, that is the beauty in the cell, music
in time, loss like water, the garden of
our way, entering the trees, an evening
of twilight where there is always
more to be loved, of your life bending like
twilight over the corn stalks
forever.